World Beat Fun

Multicultural and Contemporary Rhythms for K-8 Classrooms

By Zig Wajler

All songs written and recorded by Zig Wajler
Special Character Voices: Cindy Wajler
Editor: Gayle Giese
Art Cover Design and Layout: Lisa Greene Mane
Text Editor: Nadine DeMarco
Production Coordinator: Sharon Marlow

Zig has earned endorsements and thanks Sabian Cymbals, Pearl Drums and Pearl Percussion, Pro-Mark Drumsticks, and Zendrum.

For more information on HANDS ON WITH ZIG programs, please visit www.handsonwithzig.com.

Songs and recorded tracks used by permission © 2001 Zigsgottabashmusic
All Rights Reserved

Foreword

Zig Wajler has a very special place among drummers. I have worked with hundreds of Sabian endorsers and clinicians throughout my years, and he is the only one for whom we had to create a special category. When we first started working with Zig, he was the drummer for two separate bands that play music for young people: The Animal Band and Kat McCool. We couldn't classify him in our records with the rock, jazz, or classical drummers; he was simply an excellent musician who loved playing for kids.

When he told me he was interested in joining a Sabian-sponsored program that supports professional drummers playing in public schools, I was pleased. When he quickly became the most active member, I was not surprised. And when he had to move on because the work he was doing far surpassed the reach of the program, I was thrilled, not just for Sabian, which had always hoped that the drummers involved would grow beyond our program, and not just for Zig, who has become one of America's most original and dynamic music educators. I was thrilled for the many kids who get to see Zig play, who get to clap along, and who get to go onstage and play the percussion instruments. As you might expect, the event is called *Hands On With Zig*.

Every kid should get to see *Hands On With Zig*. Over a million have already, but there is only one Zig, and only 365 days in a year. In the meantime, I hope this book can make the wait more fun!

Bill Zildjian
Sabian, Ltd.

From the Author

This book is dedicated to the memory of Marion Sarno Johnson, Frank Konopka, Stanislava Wajler, and Harold Bachrack.

Special and never-ending thanks to my wife Cindy, my parents Jean and Zygmunt, and my sisters Renata, Bonita, Laura, and their families. Extra special thanks to Willy, Zach, and Nikki. Thanks also to Gayle Giese for providing me with this wonderful opportunity to share my music with young people.

A huge THANK YOU to all the supporters of my programs.

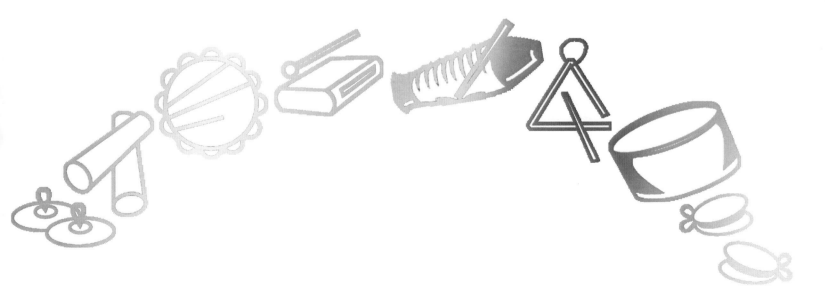

World Beat Fun

Contents

Overview

This book is based on the multicultural school program *Hands On With Zig,* an interactive educational experience that relates to the National Standards for Music and Technology. The seven play-along songs provide opportunities to interact with world music styles and contemporary themes. Students will enjoy Zig's 74 cool CD tracks. Use the *Play-Along With Zig Rhythm Track* to introduce each song.

Each song offers several rhythm parts that vary in difficulty. Some are simple enough for kindergarteners and first-graders, while others will challenge fifth-graders. The call-and-response CD tracks allow these songs to be taught by rote, and the reproducible music reinforces the reading of rhythms. A list of suggested classroom percussion instruments also appears, but feel free to substitute them with what you have available. There are different difficulty levels of rhythm parts from which to choose in each song; select the ones that make sense for your students. Any combination of parts can be played together with or without the CD to form a rhythm ensemble.

Benefits for Classroom Students

1. Learn to maintain a steady beat.
2. Experience various styles of music.
3. Discover various sounds from diverse cultures.
4. Reinforce note values and reading of rhythms.
5. Perform call-and-response rhythms as ostinatos.
6. Play independent rhythms in an ensemble.
7. Teach simple song forms.
8. Create multicultural awareness.
9. Have hands-on fun with music!

Recommended Rhythm Instruments

Each play-along song has a list of recommended instruments included on the music that are musically appropriate for that song. Feel free to substitute available classroom instruments, and you may want to add electronic keyboard percussion, but this is entirely optional. A combination of acoustic and electronic sounds can be used for any song.

Common Classroom Instruments Suggested

Bongos, castanets, claves, congas, cowbell, finger cymbals, hand drum, rhythm sticks, triangle, woodblock, guiro, maracas, ratchet, shakers, sleigh bells, cymbal, tambourine, sand blocks.

Additional Classroom Instruments (optional)
Agogo bell, bass drum, bell tree, cabasa, chimes, slapstick, snare drum, temple blocks, vibraslap.

General MIDI Electronic Percussion (optional)

Note #	Sound	Note #	Sound
35–36	bass drum	38	snare drum
39	hand clap	40	electronic snare
42	closed hi-hat	45	tom-tom
49	crash cymbal	51	ride cymbal
54	tambourine	5	cowbell
58	vibraslap	60–61	bongos
62–64	congas	65–66	timbales
69	cabasa	70	maracas
73–74	guiro	75	claves
76–77	woodblock	80–81	triangle

Far East Medley
(Asian)

 through

Teaching Suggestions

With Call-and-Response CD Tracks

1. Locate Asia and then China and Japan on a globe or world map. Ask children to tell what they know about these parts of the world.
2. To familiarize students with "Far East Medley," play CD Track 10 and invite students to patsch along to the steady beat. Ask students to describe scenes the music makes them imagine.
3. Make an overhead transparency of the call-and-response visual or photocopy and enlarge, or draw the one-measure rhythm for line 1 (finger cymbals) on the board.
4. Pointing to the rhythm notation, have students speak (when doing any pattern, use TA-A for half notes, TA for quarter notes, and TI for eighth notes or other rhythm language of your choice) and then clap the one-measure rhythm pattern.
5. Call-and-response: Clap or patsch the rhythm and then have all students respond.
6. Repeat this rhythm-learning process with all eight rhythms shown on the call-and-response visual or only those you have chosen for your class. Note that the bottom two lines have difficult rhythms for elementary students. Feel free to omit these or give them to more skilled students. Some teachers are very effective teaching new rhythms first with words or rhymes. For instance, to teach ♪♩ ╲ ♪ ♪ ♩ ♩, speak in this rhythm: *I want to boogie now.* Then transfer the speaking to patsching,   and then playing the instruments.
7. Assign instruments to each student; the instruments on the call-and-response visual are only suggestions. Refer to the call-and-response visual to note the difficulty of the rhythm as you are making assignments. Substitute other classroom instruments as needed.
8. Use the call-and-response CD Tracks 1–8 to practice the rhythms you have chosen. Point to the visual to help students see where to play. The CD tracks repeat each line one time.

Performance Suggestions

For *Play-Along-With-Zig* CD Tracks

1. CD Track 9 allows your students to play along with Zig's cool recording with the two-measure hi-hat click and voice count-off as your cue. CD Track 10 includes Zig's original rhythms, which your students can play along with once they are comfortable playing along with Track 9. Track 10 may also be used as a listening track to get the students excited about the song.
2. Use each call-and-response rhythm as an ostinato (repeated phrase) throughout the CD selection and/or assign groups of students (two or more students per group) to each section of the piece, following the Form Visual, with each group playing its part in unison with the others. For example:
    Intro: Finger Cymbals and Cymbal (Suspended) Players Only (lines 1 and 2 on call-and-response visual).
    A Section: Group 1: Finger Cymbals, Cymbal, Triangle, Castanets (lines 1–4).
    B Section: Group 2: Claves, Woodblock, Rhythm Sticks, Hand Drum (lines 5–8).
    C Section: Everyone.
    Outro: Finger Cymbals and Cymbal (Suspended) Players Only again.
3. Rehearse each group alone.
4. Use the Form Visual (copy onto a transparency) to put the sections together. Play along with CD Track 9 or 10.
5. Give students a chance to play other instruments and experiment with different instrument combinations. Which do your students think sounds best?

Visual

Far East Medley

Call-and-Response Rhythms

Students can play along with the eight call-and-response FAR EAST MEDLEY CD tracks.

The Call = notated measure   The Response = students play

♩ = 114

Track 1 — Finger Cymbals

Track 2 — Cymbal

Track 3 — Triangle

Track 4 — Castanets

Track 5 — Claves

Track 6 — Woodblock

Track 7 — Rhythm Sticks*

Track 8 — Hand Drum or Bass Drum

(Each staff alternates "notated measure" with "Students play")

* Or play on rim of snare drum.

Form Visual

Far East Medley

Track 9   Track 10

♩ = 114
Click track count-off

$\frac{4}{4}$

Intro

Single–note string melody

A

Guchin* melody

B

Oriental fiddle

C

Oriental flutes

Two Oriental flutes in harmony

Outro

Guchin melody

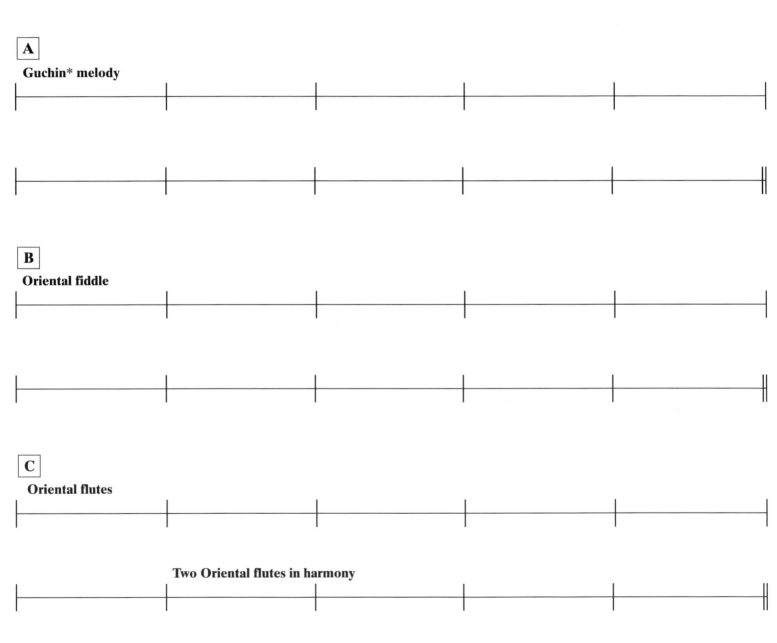

* Also known as the qin, this 7-string fretless zither is one of the oldest Chinese instruments.

Desert Theme
(Middle Eastern)

 through

Teaching Suggestions

With Call-and-Response CD Tracks

1. Locate Egypt, India, Turkey, Afghanistan, and Pakistan on a globe or world map. Discuss the terrain of these regions.
2. To familiarize students with "Desert Theme," play CD Track 20 and invite students to pretend to play drum sticks (in the air) to the steady beat. Invite them to imagine a Middle Eastern scene. What do they see? Caravans? Camels? Listen again, if desired, and have everyone move about the room to the steady beat.
3. Make an overhead transparency of the call-and-response visual or photocopy and enlarge, or draw the one-measure rhythm for line 1 (triangle) on the board.
4. Pointing to the rhythm notation, have students speak (TA TA rest rest) and then clap the one-measure rhythm pattern.
5. Call-and-response: Clap or patsch the rhythm and then have all students respond.
6. Repeat this rhythm-learning process with all eight rhythms shown on the call-and-response visual or only those you have chosen for your class. Note that rhythms on the bottom four lines are more difficult. Feel free to omit these or assign them to more skilled students.
7. Assign instruments to each student; the instruments on the call-and-response visual are only suggestions. Refer to the call-and-response visual to note the difficulty of the rhythm as you are making assignments. Substitute other classroom instruments as needed.
8. Use the call-and-response CD Tracks 11–18 to practice the rhythms you have chosen. Point to the visual to help students see where to play. The CD tracks repeat each line one time.

Performance Suggestions

For *Play-Along-With-Zig* CD Tracks

1. CD Track 19 allows your students to play along with Zig's cool recording with the two-measure hi-hat click/metronome and voice count-off as your cue. CD Track 20 includes Zig's original rhythms, which your students can play along with once they are comfortable playing along with Track 19. Track 20 may also be used as a listening track to get the students excited about the song.
2. Use each call-and-response rhythm as an ostinato (repeated phrase) throughout the CD selection and/or assign groups of students to each section of the piece, following the Form Visual, with each group playing its part in unison with the others. For example:
   A Section: Triangle, Maracas, Cymbal, Rhythm Sticks Players Only (lines 1, 4, 5, and 8 on the call-and-response visual).
   B Section: Woodblock, Finger Cymbals, Hand Drum, Tambourine Players Only (lines 2, 3, 6, and 7).
3. Rehearse each of the two groups separately.
4. Use the Form Visual (copy onto a transparency) to put the sections together and play along with CD Track 19 or 20.
5. Give students a chance to play other instruments and experiment with different instrument combinations. Have the **A** Section listen to the **B** Section and comment on their ensemble playing: *Was everyone together?* Then have the **B** Section listen to the **A** Section and describe their ensemble work.

Visual

Desert Theme

Call-and-Response Rhythms

Students can play along with the eight call-and-response DESERT THEME CD tracks.

The Call = notated measure   The Response = students play

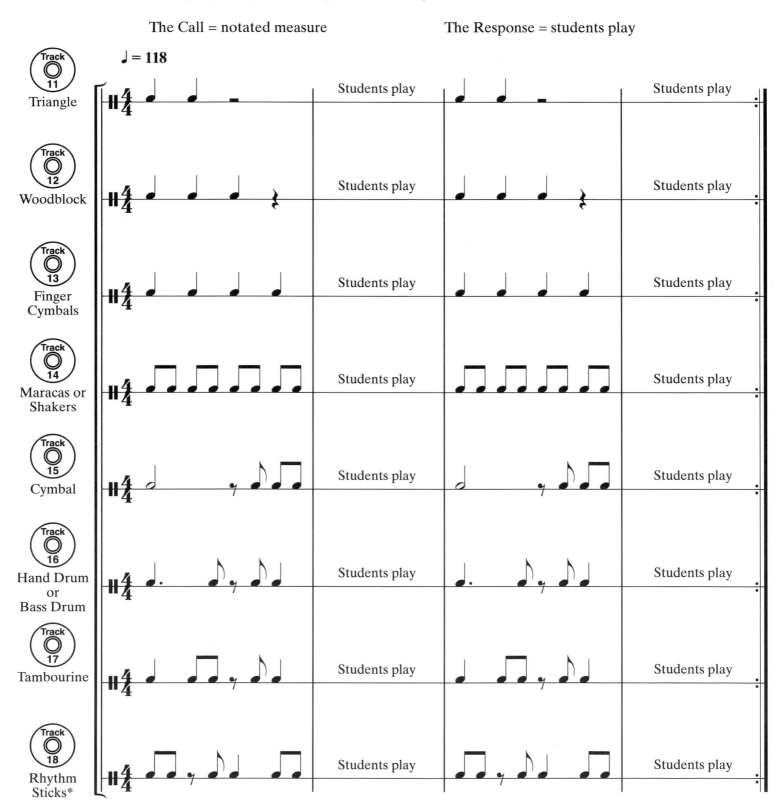

* Or play on rim of snare drum.

Form Visual

Desert Theme

Track 19

Track 20

♩ = 118
Click track count-off

A

Bass

4/4

Keyboard rhythm

Keyboards

End of A is cued by voices and descending Keyboard part.

*Oo*_____

B

String melody   **Guitar**

Keyboard rhythm   **Orchestra hit**   **Orchestra hit**

Guitar   **Turntable**   **4 Loud Orchestra hits**

Keyboard rhythm

African Dance
(Gahu* from Ghana)

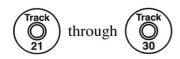 through

Teaching Suggestions

With Call-and-Response CD Tracks

1. Locate Africa and then Ghana on a world map or globe.
2. To familiarize students with "African Dance," play CD Track 32 and invite students to dance/walk to the steady beat. As they move, have them imagine an African Ghana celebration and describe the scene.
3. Make an overhead transparency of the call-and-response visual or photocopy and enlarge, or draw the one-measure rhythm for line 1 (triangle) on the board.
4. Pointing to the rhythm notation, have students speak (TA-A-A-A for the whole note) and then clap (clap on the first TA then hold hands together and pulse them on the next three beats) the one-measure rhythm pattern.
5. Call-and-response: Clap or patsch the rhythm and then have all students respond.
6. Repeat this rhythm-learning process with all ten rhythms shown on the call-and-response visual or only those you have chosen for your class. Note that rhythms on the bottom three lines are more difficult. Feel free to omit these or assign them to more skilled students.
7. Assign instruments to each student; the instruments on the call-and-response visual are only suggestions. Refer to the call-and-response visual to note the difficulty of the rhythm as you are making assignments. Substitute other classroom instruments as needed.
8. Use the call-and-response CD Tracks 21–30 to practice the rhythms you have chosen. Point to the visual to help students see where to play. The CD tracks repeat each line one time.

Performance Suggestions

For *Play-Along-With-Zig* CD Tracks

1. CD Track 31 allows your students to play along with Zig's cool recording with the two-measure hi-hat click/metronome and voice count-off as your cue. CD Track 32 includes Zig's original rhythms, which your students can play along with once they are comfortable playing along with Track 31. Track 32 may also be used as a listening track to get the students excited about the song.
2. Use each call-and-response rhythm as an ostinato (repeated phrase) throughout the CD selection and/or assign groups of students to each section of the piece, following the Form Visual, with each group playing its part in unison with the others. For example:

    A Section: Triangle, Conga, and Claves Players Only (lines 1, 3, and 5 on the call-and-response visual).
    B Section: Cowbell 1, Castanets, and Bongo Players Only (lines 2, 6, and 8).
    C Section: Cowbell 2, Rhythm Sticks, and Tambourine Players Only (lines 4, 7, and 10).
    Outro: Hand Drum Only (line 9); optionally, fade out.
3. Rehearse each of the groups separately.
4. Use the Form Visual (copy onto a transparency) to put the sections together and play along with CD tracks 31 or 32.
5. Give students a chance to play other instruments and experiment with different instrument combinations. Have all four sections rate each other's playing.

*from the Ewe tribe

Visual

African Dance

Call-and-Response Rhythms

Students can play along with the ten call-and-response AFRICAN DANCE CD tracks.

The Call = notated rhythms   The Response = students play

♩ = 114

Track	Instrument	Call	Response
21	Triangle		Students play		Students play
22	Cowbell 1		Students play		Students play
23	Conga (open sound)		Students play		Students play
24	Cowbell 2		Students play		Students play
25	Claves		Students play		Students play
26	Castanets		Students play		Students play
27	Rhythm Sticks*		Students play		Students play
28	High Bongo		Students play		Students play
29	Hand Drum or Bass Drum		Students play		Students play
30	Tambourine		Students play		Students play

* Or play on rim of snare drum.

Form Visual

African Dance

Track 31 Track 32

♩ = 114
Click track count-off

$\frac{4}{4}$

A Solo kalimba*

Two kalimbas

B

Udu** and jungle

C

slightly faster
Bass line
Loud sound effect

Rattles/shakers Bass   Bass

Outro

Bass Fill

Loud sound effect
and shakers

* African thumb piano; its wooden or metal keys are plucked with the thumbs and fingers.
  In Africa, the kalimba is most often used to accompany singing.
** Clay pot

Native American Song
(Traditional Native American with Hip-Hop)

Teaching Suggestions

With Call-and-Response CD Tracks in 3/4 and in 4/4

3/4 Meter (Track 33) through (Track 37)

4/4 Meter (Track 38) through (Track 42)

1. Ask students where Native Americans live. *Which tribal nations live in your state?* Identify on a globe or world map where different tribes live or lived. (For example, the Seminole Tribe lives in Florida.)
2. To familiarize students with "Native American Song," play CD Track 44 and invite students to listen for the steady drum beat and patsch with that beat.
3. Make an overhead transparency of the call-and-response visual or photocopy and enlarge, or draw the one-measure rhythm for line 1 in 3/4 (finger cymbals) on the board. This rhythm is a dotted half note; if you have not taught this yet, feel free to omit line 1 and start with the pattern on line 2.
4. Pointing to the rhythm notation, have students speak (TA-A-A for the dotted half note) and then clap the one-measure rhythm pattern (clap on the first TA and then hold hands together and pulse them on the next two beats).
5. Call-and-response: Clap or patsch the rhythm and then have all students respond.
6. Repeat this rhythm-learning process with all ten rhythms shown on the call-and-response visual (including the five 4/4 patterns) or only those you have chosen for your class. Note that the line 2 and line 4 rhythms in 4/4 are more difficult. Feel free to omit these or assign them to more skilled students.
7. Assign instruments to each student; the instruments on the call-and-response visual are only suggestions. Refer to the call-and-response visual to note the difficulty of the rhythm as you are making assignments. Substitute other classroom instruments as needed.
8. Use the call-and-response CD Tracks 33–42 to practice the rhythms you have chosen. Point to the visual to help students see where to play. The CD tracks repeat each line one time.

Performance Suggestions

For *Play-Along-With-Zig* CD Tracks

1. CD Track 43 allows your students to play along with Zig's cool recording with the two-measure (3/4) hi-hat click/metronome and voice count-off as your cue. CD Track 44 includes Zig's original rhythms, which your students can play along with once they are comfortable playing along with Track 43. Track 43 may also be used as a listening track to get the students excited about the song.
2. Use each 3/4 call-and-response rhythm as an ostinato (repeated phrase) throughout the 3/4 parts of the CD; use the 4/4 rhythms for the final **C** section of the recording. Then, assign groups of students to each section of the piece, following the Form Visual, with each group playing its part in unison with the others. For example:
   A Section (3/4): Finger Cymbals, Shaker, and Conga Players Only (lines 1, 3, and 5 on the 3/4 call-and-response visual).
   B Section (3/4): Tambourine and Rhythm Sticks Players Only (lines 2 and 4 or the 3/4 visual).
   C Section (4/4): Sleigh Bells, Finger Cymbals, Claves, Hand Drum, Rhythm Sticks Players (all 5 lines on the 4/4 visual). On the CD tracks, the new tempo beginning at the C section is faster: ♩ = 108.
3. Rehearse each of the groups separately.
4. Use the Form Visual (copy onto a transparency) to put the sections together and play along with CD Track 43 or 44.
5. Give students a chance to play other instruments and experiment with different instrument combinations. Have all four sections rate each other's ensemble playing.

Visual

Native American Song

Call-and-Response ¾ Rhythms

Call-and-response rhythms on Tracks 33–37 are in ¾ time.

Students can play along with the ten call-and-response NATIVE AMERICAN SONG CD tracks.

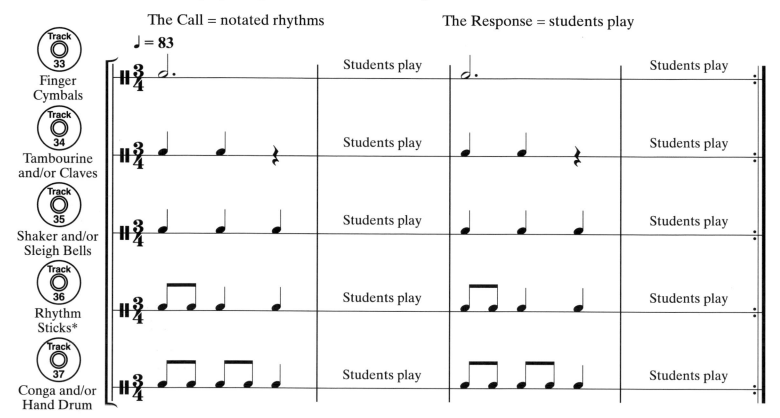

Call-and-Response 4/4 Rhythms

Call-and-response rhythms on Tracks 38–42 are in 4/4 time.

* Or play on rim of snare drum.

Form Visual

Native American Song

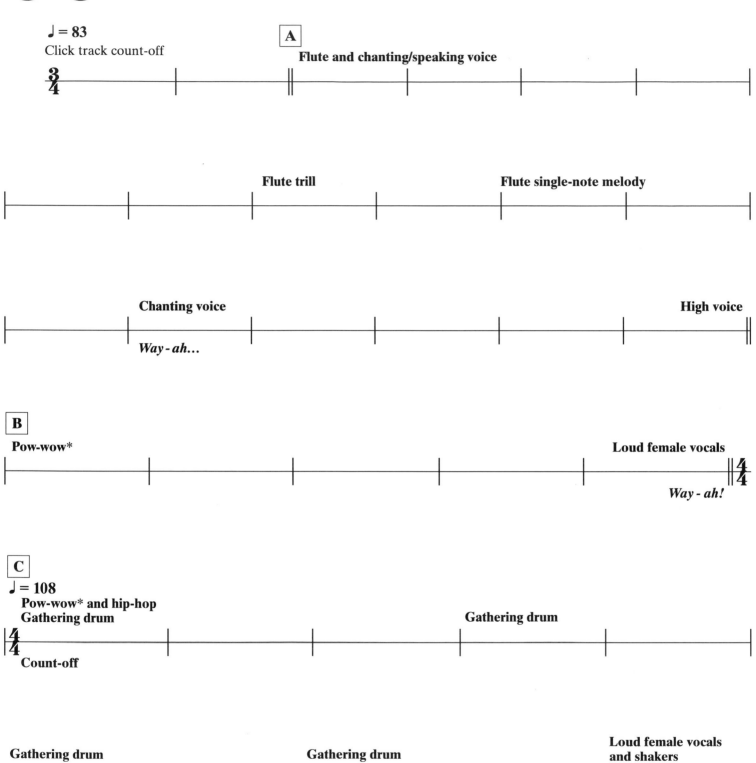

♩ = 83
Click track count-off

3/4

A

Flute and chanting/speaking voice

Flute trill   **Flute single-note melody**

Chanting voice   **High voice**

Way - ah...

B

Pow-wow*   **Loud female vocals**

4/4

Way - ah!

C

♩ = 108

Pow-wow* and hip-hop
Gathering drum   **Gathering drum**

4/4

Count-off

Gathering drum   **Gathering drum**   **Loud female vocals and shakers**

Way - ah!

* A pow-wow is a ceremonial gathering. Usually "gathering" drums keep the steady beat.
   A large, low-pitched gathering drum would usually be struck with hands or mallets by several players.

America Rocks
(North American Rock)

 through

Teaching Suggestions

With Call-and-Response CD Tracks

1. Locate several major American cities on the globe or map of the U.S. Ask students which cities make them think of jazz or the blues. Locate those cities. Ask them which cities, if any, make them think of American rock. Locate those cities. Ask students if they can name any rock artists. *What types of electric instruments might be used in a modern rock band?*

2. To familiarize students with "America Rocks," play CD Track 54 and invite students to strum the air electric guitar to the steady beat around :20. As they move, have them imagine playing in a rock band.

3. Make an overhead transparency of the call-and-response visual or photocopy and enlarge, or draw the one-measure rhythm for line 1 (tambourine or claves) on the board.

4. Pointing to the rhythm notation, have students speak (rest TA rest TA) and then clap the one-measure rhythm pattern, putting hands in the air on each rest.

5. Call-and-response: Clap or patsch the rhythm and then have all students respond.

6. Repeat this rhythm-learning process with all eight rhythms shown on the call-and-response visual or only those you have chosen for your class. Note that rhythms on the bottom three lines are more difficult. Feel free to omit these or assign them to more skilled students. Skilled students will find the sixteenth-note rhythms to be a fun challenge.

7. Assign instruments to each student; the instruments on the call-and-response visual are only suggestions. Refer to the call-and-response visual to note the difficulty of the rhythm as you are making assignments. Substitute other classroom instruments as needed.

8. Use the call-and-response CD Tracks 45–52 to practice the rhythms you have chosen. Point to the visual to help students see where to play. The CD tracks repeat each line one time.

Performance Suggestions

For *Play-Along-With-Zig* CD Tracks

1. CD Track 53 allows your students to play along with Zig's cool recording with the two-measure hi-hat click/metronome and voice count-off as your cue. CD Track 54 includes Zig's original rhythms, which your students can play along with once they are comfortable playing along with Track 53. Track 54 may also be used as a listening track to get the students excited about the song.

2. Use each call-and-response rhythm as an ostinato (repeated phrase) throughout the CD selection and/or assign groups of students to each section of the piece, following the Form Visual, with each group playing its part in unison with the others. For example:

   A Section: Cowbell and Conga Players Only (lines 4 and 6 on the call-and-response visual).
   B Section: Tambourine, Cymbal, and Rhythm Stick Players Only (lines 1, 2, and 7).
   A Section: Maracas, Hand Drum, and Bongo Players Only (lines 3, 5, and 8).

3. Rehearse each of the sections separately.

4. Use the Form Visual (copy onto a transparency) to put the sections together and play along with CD Track 53 or 54.

5. Give students a chance to play other instruments and experiment with different instrument combinations. Have the **A** and **B** sections rate each other's ensemble playing.

Visual

America Rocks

Call-and-Response Rhythms

Students can play along with the eight call-and-response AMERICA ROCKS CD tracks.

The Call = notated measure   The Response = students play

♩ = 120

Track 45 — Tambourine and/or Claves

Track 46 — Cymbal

Track 47 — Maracas and/or Shaker

Track 48 — Cowbell

Track 49 — Hand Drum

Track 50 — Conga

Track 51 — Rhythm Sticks*

Track 52 — Bongos

Students play (repeated in each measure)

* Or play on rim of snare drum.

Form Visual

America Rocks

Track 53   Track 54

♩ = 120
Click track count-off

$\frac{4}{4}$

A

Heavy rhythm guitar   **Guitar lead**

B

Chord changes and guitar lead

Guitar lead

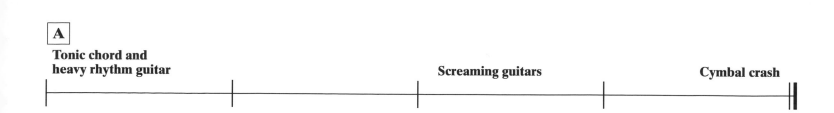

A

**Tonic chord and
heavy rhythm guitar**   **Screaming guitars**   **Cymbal crash**

Trip to the Amazon and the Ocean
(Sounds of the Rain Forest)*

 through

Teaching Suggestions

With Call-and-Response CD Tracks

1. Locate the Brazilian rain forest and the wide Amazon River on a world map or globe. Discuss the importance of rain forests and the medicines and foods they supply. *What do we breathe that comes from the trees? Are rain forests a unique habitat? What animals and plants live there? Could these animals and plants survive elsewhere?*

2. To familiarize students with "Trip to the Amazon and the Ocean," play CD Track 64 and invite students to listen for the animals they hear. Invite them to imagine a walk through the rain forest or a trip down the Amazon River. Listen again, if desired, and have students patsch the steady beat; ask one student to play a rainstick if you have one.

3. This song exercise differs from others in this book because it is more an exercise in listening and communicating than in playing exact rhythm patterns. Each rhythm on the call-and-response visual is notated as a whole note with a tremolo indication above it. Students can improvise any rhythm they like for four beats. Challenge them to create some good ones!

4. Call-and-response: Demonstrate by doing the call yourself and having students respond to you. Then, select some students to choose rhythms to which the rest of the class will respond. Make sure the student doing the call creates a rhythm that lasts only four beats; the student may use both sound and silence (rests)! Write eight of these rhythm patterns on the board and label them #1–#8.

5. Assign instruments and a pattern to each student. Substitute other classroom instruments as needed. See the Instrument Playing suggestions below.

6. Use the call-and-response CD Tracks 55–62 to practice the rhythms you have chosen. (On the CD, a tremolo occurs for four beats.) The CD tracks repeat each line on the call-and-response visual one time.

Instrument Playing Suggestions

- Triangle should be played lightly inside its bars with a back-and-forth motion.
- Woodblock can be played with two mallets producing a slow to fast roll.
- Students could use two mallets on a cymbal to create a more sustained sound like a roll. If only concert-style cymbals are available, have one student hold the cymbal horizontally, allowing another student to play upon it.
- Claves can play a series of notes starting very fast and then rapidly slowing down.
- Bongos and conga can be played with two hands producing a slow to fast roll.
- Guiro can be scraped slowly over a count of two beats or quickly with back-and-forth strokes.
- Shakers can be held vertically and shaken quickly back and forth to produce a rattle-like sound.

Performance Suggestions

For *Play-Along-With-Zig* CD Tracks

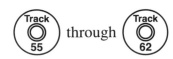

1. CD Track 63 allows your students to play along with Zig's cool recording with the two-measure hi-hat click/metronome and voice count-off as your cue. CD Track 64 includes Zig's original rhythms, which your students can play along with once they are comfortable playing along with Track 63. Track 64 may also be used as a listening track to get the students excited about the song.

2. Use the eight call-and-response rhythms your class created as an ostinato (repeated phrase) throughout the CD selection and/or assign soloists or groups of students to each section or measure of the piece, following the Form Visual, with each group playing its part in an order that you decide. You can label the parts on the Form Visual. Ask students to listen for space, sometimes using one solo instrument or group for the duration

of a measure, creating a color or special effect. This song is in a slow 4/4.

Examples for Instrument Distribution (these are only suggestions):

A Section: Triangle and Woodblock (Lines 1 and 2: triangle could play for three measures and then woodblock for three measures).

B Section: Cymbal, Claves, and Bongos (Lines 3, 4, and 5: cymbal for one measure, claves for two measures, and then bongos for two measures).

C Section: Conga, Guiro, and Shakers (Lines 6, 7, and 8: each could play a solo for two measures, and then they all could play together for two measures for a total of eight measures).

Outro: Solo Guiro for two measures, Solo Conga for two measures, Solo Triangle for two measures, and then Solo Cymbal that fades out for final two measures.

3. Follow the Form Visual with the parts you have labeled to put the sections together. Point to the visual to cue the different groups of players. Play along with CD Track 63 or 64.

4. Give students a chance to play other instruments and experiment with different instrument combinations.

---

* For a complete study unit, CD, and cross-curricular musical for Grades 3–8 about the rain forest and endangered species, ask your music or school supply store for *Help the Animals!* (BMR06016CD) from Warner Bros. Publications, 15800 NW 48th Ave., Miami, FL 33014; 305/620-1500.

Visual

Trip to the Amazon and the Ocean

Call-and-Response Rhythms

Students can play along with the eight call-and-response TRIP TO THE AMAZON AND THE OCEAN CD tracks.

The Call = notated measure   The Response = students play

♩ = 60

Track 55 Triangle — Students play / Students play

Track 56 Woodblock — Students play / Students play

Track 57 Cymbal — Students play / Students play

Track 58 Claves — Students play / Students play
fast to slow roll   *fast to slow roll*

Track 59 Bongos — Students play / Students play
slow to fast roll   *slow to fast roll*

Track 60 Conga — Students play / Students play
slow to fast roll   *slow to fast roll*

Track 61 Guiro — Students play / Students play

Track 62 Shakers — Students play / Students play

Form Visual

Trip to the Amazon and the Ocean

Track 63　Track 64

♩ = 60
Click track count-off

A Birds, crickets, tree-frogs　　Owl

B
Rain forest and ocean roar　　　　　　Ocean roar　　　Ocean waves

C
Dolphins and whales　　　　　　Whales　　　Splashing, waves

Ocean roar

Outro
Flute and voices

you can help me save the earth...

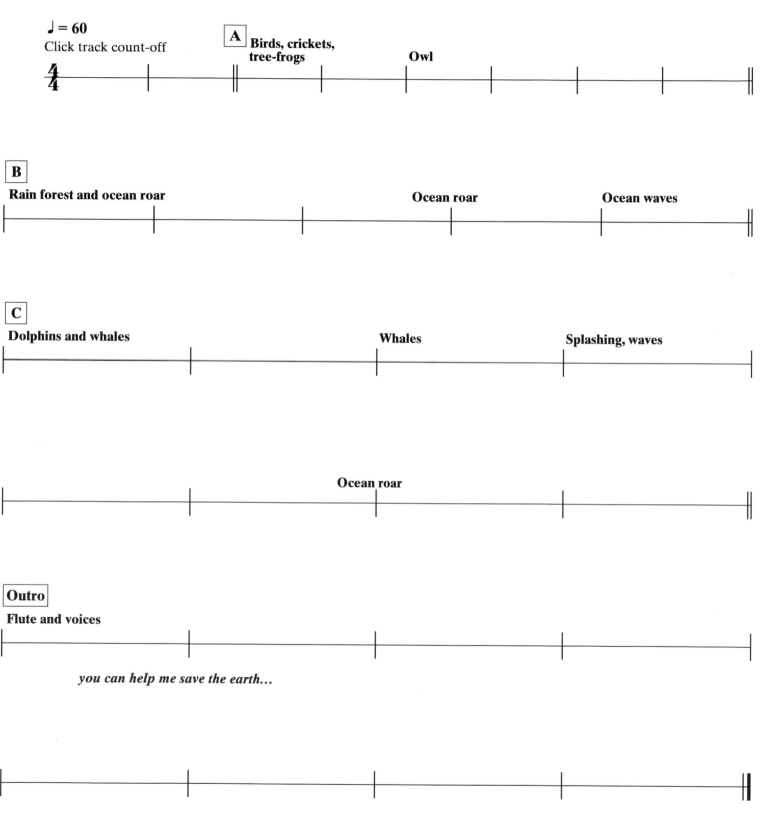

3-2 Cuban Salsa
(Afro-Caribbean)

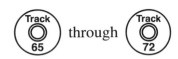 through

Teaching Suggestions

With Call-and-Response CD Tracks

1. Locate the island of Cuba on a world map or globe. *Can anyone name a musical artist who comes from Cuba?*
2. To familiarize students with "3-2 Cuban Salsa," play CD Track 74 and invite students to dance/walk to the steady beat. As they move, have them imagine a tropical island beach scene.
3. Make an overhead transparency of the call-and-response visual or photocopy and enlarge, or draw the one-measure rhythm for line 1 (Cowbell 1) on the board.
4. Pointing to the rhythm notation, have students speak (TA-A TA-A for the two half notes) and then clap the one-measure rhythm pattern. Notice that this piece is shown in cut-time (2/2), but you may count it in fast 4/4. The fast tempo and use of cut-time make this piece challenging!
5. Call-and-response: Clap or patsch the rhythm and then have all students respond.
6. Repeat this rhythm-learning process with all eight rhythms shown on the call-and-response visual or only those you have chosen for your class.
7. Assign instruments to each student; the instruments on the call-and-response visual are only suggestions. Refer to the call-and-response visual to note the difficulty of the rhythm as you are making assignments. Substitute other classroom instruments as needed.
8. Use the call-and-response CD Tracks 65–72 to practice the rhythms you have chosen. Point to the visual to help students see where to play. The CD tracks repeat each line one time.

Performance Suggestions

For *Play-Along-With-Zig* CD Tracks

1. **Salsa** is a blend of various Latin musical styles.
2. The claves' (two round, thick wooden sticks) syncopated two-measure rhythm is the key to Latin music.
3. Allow your students to play along with Zig's cool Track 73 or 74, listening for the four-measure hi-hat click/metronome and voice count-off as your cue. CD Track 74 includes Zig's original rhythms throughout, while Track 73 includes them in only the **A** and **Outro** sections.
4. Use each call-and-response rhythm as an ostinato (repeated phrase) throughout the CD selection and/or assign groups of students to each section of the piece, following the Form Visual, with each group playing its part in unison with the others. For example:
    > **A** Section: Cowbell 1, Rhythm Sticks, Shakers, and Guiro Players Only (lines 1, 3, 5, and 8 on the call-and-response visual). (Notice that the **A** Section is 28 measures and much longer than the other sections.)
    > **B** Section: Cowbell 2, Claves, Bongos Players Only (lines 2, 4, and 6).
    > **Outro:** Conga Solo (line 7); optionally, fade out.
5. Rehearse each of the groups separately.
6. Use the Form Visual (copy onto a transparency) to put the sections together and play along with CD Track 73 or 74.
7. Give students a chance to play other instruments and experiment with different instrument combinations.

Visual

3-2 Cuban Salsa

Call-and-Response Rhythms

Students can play along with the eight call-and-response 3-2 CUBAN SALSA CD tracks.

The Call = notated measure   The Response = students play

Track 65 — Cowbell 1

♩ = 96

Students play — Students play

Track 66 — Cowbell 2

Students play — Students play

Track 67 — Rhythm Sticks*

Students play — Students play

Track 68 — Claves Woodblock

2-measure pattern — Students play ⟶

Track 69 — Shakers and/or Maracas

Students play — Students play

Track 70 — High Bongo Low Bongo

high — low — Students play — Students play

Track 71 — Conga

closed sound — open sound — Students play — Students play

Track 72 — Guiro

long sound — short sound — Students play — Students play

* Or play on rim of snare drum.

Form Visual

3-2 Cuban Salsa

♩ = **48**
Click track count-off

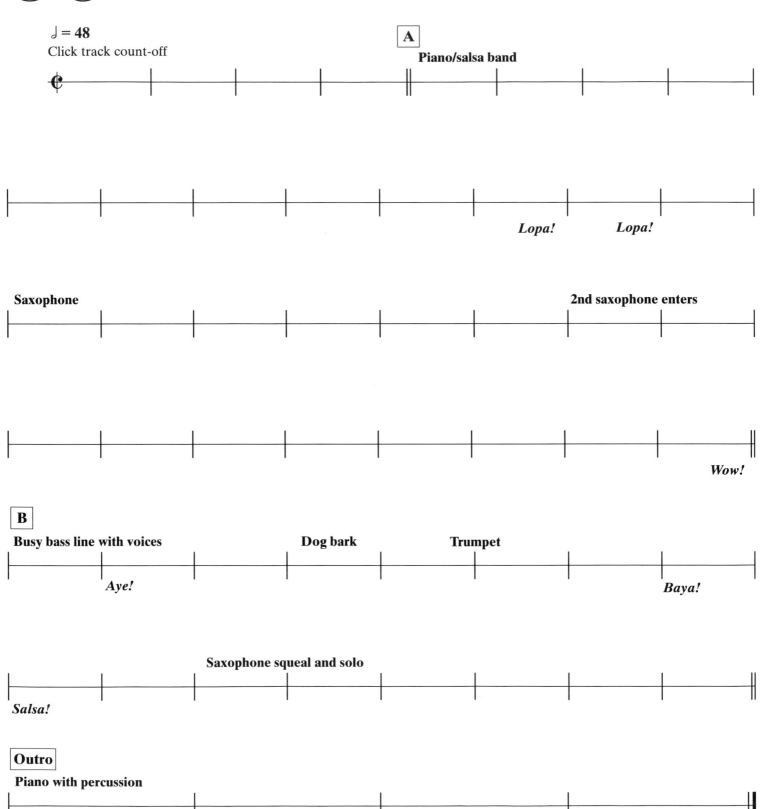

A
Piano/salsa band

Lopa!   *Lopa!*

Saxophone   **2nd saxophone enters**

Wow!

B
Busy bass line with voices   **Dog bark**   **Trumpet**

Aye!   *Baya!*

Saxophone squeal and solo

Salsa!

Outro
Piano with percussion

Adios.

About the Author

Zig Wajler is popular for his school presentations entitled *Hands On With Zig* in which he integrates music technology with percussion and multicultural themes to create an exciting learning environment for students. Zig's performance credits include ABC, TNN, VH-1, VH-1 Save the Music, PBS, FOX, Disney, and Comedy Central. He is an award-winning instructor with the Percussive Arts Society/Sabian Scholarship, has received a Nashville Nammy with The Animal Band, and has appeared in *Modern Drummer* and *DRUM!* magazines. Zig also serves as a committee member for the MARS Music Foundation and Be True Arts Foundation. Zig's other percussion performance credentials include *Terminator 2, For the Boys, LA Story, Sideout,* Shari Lewis and Lambchop, Thomas the Tank Engine, Bob McGrath ("Sesame Street"), Snoopy, Trout Fishing in America, The Moffatts, The Animal Band, Shawn Camp, Kat McKool, Wade Hayes, Marty Brown, Johnny Russell, Steve Earle, Arlon Roth, the Torrance Symphony, Chonda Pierce, and James Payne. Zig has been a presenter for the Tennessee Library Association, The Helen Keller School, Odyssey of the Minds, The SAF, Meet the Composer, Arts Build Communities, and Arts 4 All.

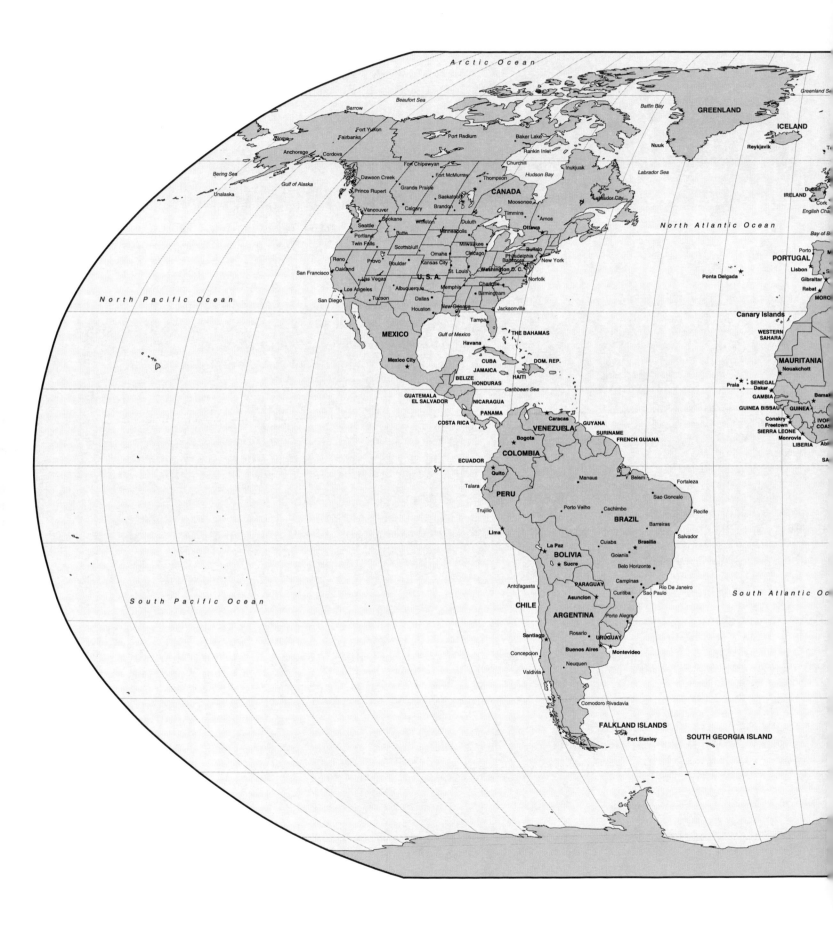

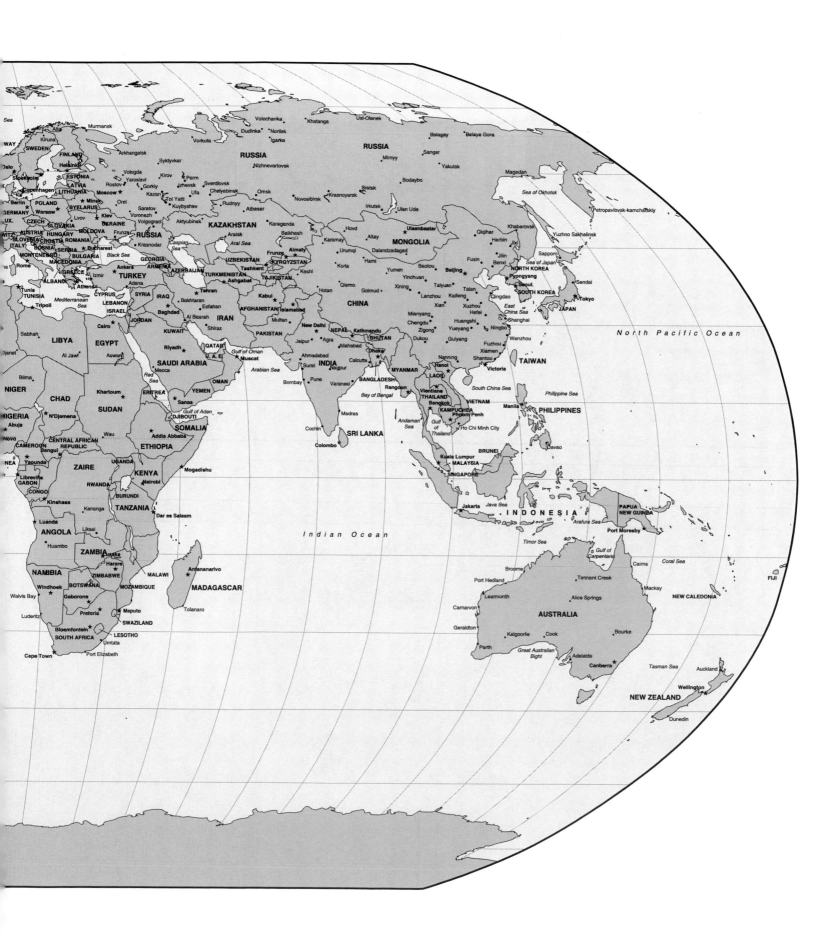